Stop Wasting Your Time As A Therapist!

Mark Bowden

ISBN: 9798743732241

Contents

1 Introduction

I help businesses of all sorts of sizes, to implement new software, to get the value out of the software they've got, and automate some of their processes. One of the areas I've done quite a bit of work on in recent years is helping therapists of various sorts.

This book is a summary of how you can stop wasting time on things you don't enjoy in your therapy business, and spend more time working on the things that you went into business to do.

I slightly provocatively titled this book "Stop Wasting Your Time As A Therapist", but hopefully, by the end of it, you'll understand where I'm going with that. I'll reassure you now that I'm absolutely *not* suggesting that the therapy you deliver is in any way a waste of time – quite the contrary. However, I do believe that there's a good chance you're wasting time when you could be practising it.

I talk to lots of clients across different business sectors, and certain things frequently come out. And I hope when you get to the end of it, you'll see how it gives you the capacity to have more clients and less stress in your own business.

If you're not a therapist, you may still find this book helpful in streamlining and automating your business, particularly if you're a tutor, a coach, or a consultant, but even if you're a builder, an engineer, or a lawyer. There are some specifics that I have included for the therapy industry but the core principles are the same ones I use when consulting across any industry.

As I write this book I become increasingly aware that whilst it is full of practical tips and advice on how to save non-productive time in your business, the single biggest obstacle to freeing yourself up to do the work you love is not practical at all. It is mindset. Many therapists I speak to are obsessed with saving the small costs in their business, and trying to do everything themselves, because it's cheaper, and they want it done "just so".

In reality, they have a far high opportunity cost by doing work that isn't client-facing, and which they usually hate, in order to save a few pounds here or there, which they could easily cover by making that time client-facing, and therefore revenue earning.

Those who can bring themselves to take a more commercial view of costs and processes are the ones who free themselves from the grind. There are investments that need to be made in order to do that, both in terms of money and time, but viewed through the lens of Return On Investment (ROI) rather than simply as costs, it quickly becomes apparent that trying to do everything yourself for free is, in fact, a false economy, and one that shackles you to the more mundane parts of your business. If you work in this way, you'll struggle to take a day off, struggle to stop doing the work your hate, and struggle to make your business a financial success.

Stepping back and making wise investments, incrementally, will allow you to release your time and move to a world where your business works for you, not the other way around. I'm not advocating spending hundreds or thousands of pounds on new tools and systems. But I am saying that if you come at this problem with a poverty mindset, always seeking to minimize what you spend, you will not break out of the cycle and enable your business to operate the way you want it to.

2 So Much Wasted Time…

My first challenge to you is this…

Why are you here?

And I don't mean, "Why are you here reading this book?"

But *why are you here as a business?*

You're here to help clients deal with some sort of problem using whatever therapy or service you're an expert in. Obviously, there is a huge range of different therapies that you may practice, and help people with different sorts of problems. But fundamentally, you're here because you want to help people using the skills that you've got.

In common with anyone who is running a purpose-led business, you probably got into it to help people and perhaps you didn't realise before you started how much other "stuff" has to happen to make what you love into a viable business. Let's be honest, some of that needs to happen even to run a business that isn't viable!

So there is a whole range of things that you're not here to do and let's think about some of those.

You're not here for some of these things...

You went into business to help customers, using the service that you are an expert in

But several things happen in your business, that take up time but don't get you paid...

- Setting up meetings and appointments

- Missed appointments

- Posting to social media

- Copying and pasting / rekeying information

- Transcribing voice or video content for articles / blogs / client notes

- Your accounts

- Getting reviews

There are several examples of things here that happen in your business that don't actually get you paid or your clients helped, they just take up your time.

Setting up appointments is fairly self-explanatory, but whether it's an appointment or a business meeting, it can require quite a bit of email tennis, trying to line up diaries, and particularly then if you have to call and reschedule anything if you have any illness or you need to reorganise, can get really quite time-consuming.

Just when you think you have it nailed, there's the issue of missed appointments. This is a varying problem depending on a number of things, but pure and simple: missed appointments waste time. Clearly, that's time that you were blocked out to be getting paid by a client and potentially you're twiddling your thumbs. That's obviously not a great business strategy!

The time you're spending doing things like your accounts (and obviously, depending on the size of your business you may have a have bookkeeper) is also time spent doing something which is not directly getting you paid. This includes all of the activity around doing your accounts, the mechanics of getting paid, tracking all of the financial performance of your business and logging that information. Unless you're an accountant, you probably didn't go into business to do that. There's a good chance you don't enjoy it, and the time you spend doing it is time you aren't delivering therapy to a client. Not core to your business, but you can't run a business without it.

And thirdly, getting reviews. Different businesses spend differing amounts of time proactively getting reviews from customers, and if you've made a serious attempt to do it, you'll know that it can be quite time-consuming. Not only that, you can have quite mixed results. Equally, a lot of the time when I speak to businesses, particularly small businesses people say *"Well, I feel very uncomfortable asking for reviews, so I just don't do it"*. But as we'll see later, they are important social proof and if you skip on doing them it will have consequences for your business in the longer term.

That's the four headline areas, but with all of those, there's a multitude of tasks underneath those headlines that need to happen... And none of them are directly getting you paid. And none of them are directly helping your clients either. They are, in essence, the administrative "stuff" that wraps around your real "value-add time" – the good that you went into business to do.

Missed Appointments

So how many appointments are missed in your business? This is going to be very different for different businesses but let's look at some statistics.

Defife, Conklin and Smith published a paper on this in 2010. They looked at 542 appointments across a range of different therapies in different settings and concluded that on average 14% of all of those were missed.

Think about how that relates to your business does that feel about right?

Of course, there will be variations depending on a wide range of factors including, the nature of your clients and therapy, your location, cost, cancellation policy and several others. However consider this average in the context that if you're doing seven appointments in a day, that's one missed appointment. Over the course of a week, that's quite a large opportunity cost and could add up to over half a day of wasted time.

This is unplanned downtime for you because these are appointments that are no shows or late cancellations - so different from the time that you may plan away from the client-side of your business, where you might have planned time to be doing training. This could be "eleventh hour" in nature and thought about in that way, even one hour per week is wasted time.

How much work does it take to set up an appointment?

This is another interesting statistic. x.ai build meeting software, and they did a survey in 2014 of 12,411 meetings globally. The question they sought to answer was how many emails were required for people to actually settle on a firm slot that could work including reschedules, and everything else. And they arrived at a figure of... *8.02*

Again, your mileage may vary – this study was across all types of meetings in all types of contexts, but even if it's only two emails for every appointment, and each takes just 2 minutes to deal with, for a 30-minute appointment, you're losing nearly 13% of your time.

It might not sound much but scale that up and it amounts to a staggering 233 hours per year – that's over 6 weeks. Even if your appointments are all an hour, that's 3 weeks when you're earning as effectively as if you were on holiday, but not having half as much fun!

If you then layer over the fact that you know that one in seven of those is being cancelled after it's been set up you're wasting a ridiculous amount of time, just on this one simple, non-revenue generating, task.

So what's it going to be?

3 weeks on the beach or 3 weeks of email tennis?

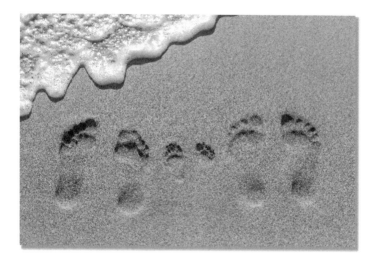

3 How To Plan

Great, so you're sold on the idea of systemising your business, and you're ready to dive straight in!

But before you do, just stop.

There are 4 phases you're going to need to work through to make this a success:

- Planning
- Understand
- Execute
- Analyse

A successful transformation is not just about doing the right thing, it's also about doing things right.

The Planning Phase

Planning is a critical first stage. Around 70% of digital transformations globally across all industries, all business sizes and all geographies fail. That is not to say that 70% of the time, the business, attempting to make the transformation fails.

However, more than seven out of every 10 attempts to radically transform a business, bringing new technology, new ways of working failed to deliver the expected benefits to that business. In some cases, the project fails to deliver anything at all. In other cases, it may deliver everything expected, but the benefits simply do not materialise. And the number one reason for failure is failure to plan. Indeed, the old adage holds very true. That to fail to plan is to plan to fail.

It is essential that rather than diving straight into the first shiny new piece of tech that you've set your eyes on and figuring out how to make it work in your business. Instead, you must approach the problem in a more logical manner and understand what you are trying to achieve in your business.

Begin this by setting objectives and key outcomes:

- What outcomes are you looking to get to?
- Are you seeking to reduce costs?
- Are you seeking to improve customer service?

- Are you seeking to increase sales or revenues?

You must have the answers to these questions before you even begin to plan. Furthermore, you must quantify those answers. It is not enough, simply to say, "I want to see an increase in sales and a reduction in costs". You need to understand enough about your business before you start this to be able to set a sensible boundary.

"I want to increase my sales by 10%"

"I want to increase my profit margin by 5%"

"I want to reduce my costs by 12%"

All of those are valid statements to make. So before you dive in any further the very first thing to do is to be very clear and specific about what a good outcome looks like for you can write it down. Write it down because you're going to come back to it at the end of this process, and you're going to ask yourself questions like

"Have I achieved this number?"

And if you have not achieved this number you're going to ask yourself

"Why did I not achieve this number?"

"What do I need to do differently to achieve this number?"

"Was the number realistic?"

If the number was realistic, where did you go wrong on the planning or the execution?

The Understand Phase

Once you've clarified the objective of your business transformation, the next key step, which again is before you even begin employing any changes in your technology or processes, is to understand your existing business. The "Understand" phase is absolutely essential.

In the Understand phase, we're going to think through the existing business that you have along three pillars. People process and technology.

Notice the order of those. So many business owners and entrepreneurs dive straight into the technology.

They start with the technology because they see a new shiny thing and they want it, so they get it, and then try to figure out how to fit it to their business.

It's the last step of the three!.

It's crucial that you understand the first two in the right order before you get there because if you do not understand the constraints that your existing business is running under and you do not understand in enough detail the processes and the problems within those processes that your existing business is running under, you may well buy the wrong solution.

A solution to solve the problem that you don't have.

Even if, by luck, you do buy the right solution for a problem that you actually do have, you may not deploy it in the most efficient way - and you may still not achieve the results that you're expecting.

Lastly, even if you do achieve the results you're expecting, you won't be able to measure it, so you won't know you've achieved those results.

Knowing you have or have not achieved the results is critical because digital transformation in a business is not a "one and done" task. It's a continuous improvement. You're going to improve parts of your business, you're going to optimise parts of your business and use new technology in your business. And when you've done all of that you're going to go right back to the start and do it again. So getting the right culture and the right mindset, around how to tackle this is critical.

In the next section, you'll learn about the key understanding activities that you need to undertake under each of the headings people process and technology work through those and be clear about how they apply in your business. Then, after you've done that you will be ready to start planning some real change in your business. The advice I give here is broadly the same irrespective of whether your business is just you operating as a therapist or when I'm talking to a client turning over £100m per year or more, because although the questions are simpler to answer when it's just you running a therapy business, *they are still the right questions to ask.*

So as you read through the following sections think about them in the context of your business, and what they mean for you. If you're a single therapist running your business without help then some of this is going to seem redundant, and indeed at this stage, it may well be. However, by actively considering it and moving on you're ensuring that it is, rather than simply forgetting (or not realizing) you need to think about it. Further, thinking about the things that larger businesses need to care about now, means that you're likely to set yourself up in the right way to grow your business sustainably and systematically.

4 People

The first pillar of the change process is People. We tackle this first because if you have issues with the people in the organisation not being fully bought into the change at some or all levels, then really the understanding of the processes and the technology choices that will be made later are really irrelevant. Without the leadership and the employees in the business being fully committed, your change is going to fail.

Leadership

Leadership is really important. If the leadership of an organisation are not completely committed, it's unlikely that any change is going to succeed. For any transformation worth undertaking there are going to be some really difficult trade-offs to be taken during the journey, and the leadership of the organisation are the ones who are going to have to take them. They are going to be a need to prioritise resources, be they people or money, between running today's business and building tomorrow's business. This means that sometimes it may be necessary to let timescales or standards slide a little in order to free up key people to help build the future organisation.

The fact is that it is highly likely that key people will not be sat there desperate to step away from the job they feel safe and secure in, to help make elements of that job redundant. They will most likely need to be gently coaxed, and in some cases more directly instructed to provide their subject matter expertise into the transformation programme. So without a leadership team that is 100% committed, and able to skilfully lead their team to buy into the future, it is almost certain that the project team will struggle to gain the knowledge required. Worse, these key subject matter experts will begin to feel that the change is being done to them, not by them, and will push back accordingly. In some cases individuals may simply feel disenfranchised by the transformation and disengage from it, becoming passengers on the journey.

However, the real worry is those who become active saboteurs. These people may well claim to be supportive on the face of it, but in fact, may be actively telling colleagues that this will never work and deliberately avoid providing their knowledge by claiming not to have the time to get involved. Without leadership support to cut through this, any change will become bogged down in trying to get the details of the current processes, or risks delivering a poor solution (which will only reinforce the "I told you it would never work" narrative) because it presses on without key details. These people are just waiting for your project to fail, to validate their conscious or unconscious view that change is never a good thing, and that it would be better if things just stayed as they are.

Furthermore, when difficult decisions need to be taken, if the leadership isn't completely on board with that vision for tomorrow, it's going to be extremely difficult for them to take those decisions and to prioritise getting to where they need to get to. If they keep putting today's issue ahead of building for tomorrow then they are doomed to repeat the same cycle without making any progress.

That said, an over-enthusiastic leadership can also have some risks – there's little point in going all in to deliver a vision of the future if getting there is going to destroy customer confidence to the point that the business simply no longer exists. Besides, overly enthusiastic leadership can lead to a highly dangerous culture within the change project where it becomes unacceptable to acknowledge that certain things are hard, late or incomplete, and in so doing the reality on the ground becomes disjointed from the situation that the leaders believe they have. Usually, this ends badly at some point – not providing the bad news as well as the good news simply defers the day or reckoning.

Whether you're running your own business or part of the leadership team of a business then the fact that you're reading this indicates that you are on the right path to having that leadership commitment, but before you start, challenge yourself and your colleagues about how willing you will be to take some hard priority choices.

Whether you are the leadership and the business, or whether you're part of a leadership team within a larger business, you've "shown up", so you're committed to making some changes in your business. And that's a great start. But be aware that there are going to be multiple times in this journey where you may well want to have to choose between the present and the future, and where saying "I want both" is not an option. If you want both, you'll likely get neither. Accept the reality of that situation now, or put down this book and go home, because nothing else I say here can save you.

Culture

The second element of People is Culture, and the impact that has on your change project is going to depend upon how big your organisation is. In a really small business with one or two people, culture is not a significant issue – if the leadership team (business owner) says this is going to happen then the likelihood is that anyone else working in the business is going to get on and make it happen.

But once you get to a dozen or more people things change and it does start to matter. It is somewhere around this number that something interesting happens to most organisations. They switch from being an organisation where everyone is implicitly pulling together to make something a success and where hard lines of demarcation often don't exist between roles, to an organisation with stricter rules and boundaries. This simply has to happen to scale beyond the initial "tribe", but can often lead to two groups of employees – the founder and their initial few hires, and then the newer recruits who have come into this more structured organisation. This can lead to all sorts of tensions between these groups, with the newer entrants seeing the original group as lacking discipline, the original group seeing the newer hires as less committed to the success of the organisation, and all sorts of inter-personal issues rooted within those two cultures. Ultimately for the business to grow further, the second culture has to win out, because otherwise the business will never really scale beyond that early tribe, but getting there can be tough for a growing business.

Unfortunately, these struggles in culture often play out in parallel to a major change in the business's systems. The introduction of these new rules and standards require it. But of course, this can also mean that the transformative work is also caught up in this wider culture war, and risks being derailed as both sides see it as a problem.

Before starting any transformation it is important to take a step back and understand the culture of the organisation. Ask yourself some questions about it and try to think about where potential issues may lie. This will allow you to plan and take pre-emptive action to avoid it.

Some key questions to ask would include:

What is the culture of your organisation?

How receptive is your organisation to change?

Next think about whether you have a handful of key people in your business who might be blockers to change because if you do, you need to get those people on board now. You must do this before they start to see this as work might threaten their job or their security, You need to bring them on board and get them excited about the future which means you need them bought into the vision before you even start to communicate it more widely. If you do this, they can help you. However, if you don't, you will find that they will be significant blockers when you get further through the change process.

These are often the same people that can become saboteurs if not handled well, but engaged and encouraged, they can also be your strongest allies because they are usually the people that really understand what happens in your organisation.

And you're not going to make this change work without them.

Skills

The final part of People is Skills. This is the more practical, more pragmatic view that you need to take within your organisation around how large the task of bringing your people up to the required skill level is likely to be.

You need to consider what skills gap you've got within the organisation, both in terms of the skills to facilitate change, and the skills your people will need when the change is complete. You're going to need to get your people to move to new ways of working. This might be as simple as what skills they need to use a new piece of software, it might be that you need to completely retrain them on how they think about and how they do their job. Whatever the answer is in your business, you need to go into this with your eyes wide open. To start that you need to have thought about the skills gap that might exist in your organisation before you even begin to plan the work.

You must consider this now, before you start, because if you don't you'll create delivery risk for your change project, and you are highly likely to find that diary management becomes a big problem towards the end of the project when you need key people to provide input on decisions, or to test a new system, whilst doing their "day jobs" and then you realise you need to send them on training as well.

By understanding the skills gap early, you have time to plan the training. However, there's also an important link to the other people considerations – if you invest in your key people early and train them with new skills, it will reduce the fear of the change and inspire at least some of them to get the project delivered and be able to use their new skills. Conversely, by leaving training late, you are creating a completely unnecessary barrier to adoption later by increasing the fear of the future, making it more likely that people will begin to worry that they are in danger of being made redundant or be replaced. You're going to have to do the training anyway, so delaying it serves little practical purpose and just causes problems.

Of course, beware of training people on something highly technical weeks or months before they need to use it without any sort of refresher. Instead aim to drip feed the knowledge of the new systems and processes to those who need it during the life of the project.

Again, if it's just you in your business, this planning is fairly easy – you will need to learn the new tools, and will most likely need some outside help to enable you to deliver a large change anyway. If it's a bigger organisation, however, you might need to do quite a bit of legwork, conducting a skills audit and developing a training plan.

But either way, capture this information now.

Where do you think there is a skills gap?

What training can you access?

How else you might be able to close it?

It's important to understand that before you go into making any significant change to your business

5 Process

The second pillar is Process, and we're going to talk a lot about process in this book. Getting the right process is probably the most important part of a successful change. You need your people to be on board, you will be using new technology. But if your process isn't right, the fundamental way that you're doing things within your business is not going to be effective.

With the wrong process, you are very likely to simply end up doing the wrong thing, only faster. Even if this doesn't lead to any customer-facing issues, it means that you will have failed to eliminate waste from your processes and in some cases, you may even have more waste. In this scenario, you'll have to increase the pace of operations just to stand still and if you do achieve a benefit, it will be a fraction of what you could have achieved with a little more effort here.

Again, we break the Process pillar out into three areas. And we start right at the top of the organisation.

Mission and Purpose

The first thing you need to challenge yourself on and think about is whether you have a clear mission for your business?

It might sound ridiculously simple. And you may say, "of course I do". But you'd be surprised how many businesses cannot articulate a clear mission statement, objective and purpose.

And if you can't do that, you don't really know what you're trying to improve, and will even struggle to define what "improve" means.

What are you trying to do better?

What will it mean to be better?

How will you know if you have achieved it?

It's really important to get that clarity of mind before you start.

If your business already has a mission statement, then that is the first thing to begin with. If you achieve the outcome you envision, does that mission still make sense? If it doesn't then it's probably not really a mission statement, more like it is an objective you're currently trying to achieve. You may need to dig deep here and think about why your business exists. What is the thing that drives the thing you do, not the thing itself?

Some great examples of this might be an online course creator. They could state that their mission is "To make courses out of all my knowledge" but really if they dig deep they will realise that they do it because they care deeply about helping people to acquire new skills so that they can live a better life, or because they want to help business owners repeat themselves less and have more time to do what they love.

Whichever it is, THAT is the essence of their real mission.

Once you understand your mission, you can begin to think about how this change aligns with and supports you in achieving that mission. But the delivery of the change should not change the mission itself. If it does, you'll need to dig some more.

You can do this by asking yourself "why?"...

Why is your business here? Is a great place to start. Once you answer that, ask "why?" that is the answer, when you answer *that*, ask again. Keep going until you get right to the bottom of what drives your business. And that is the essence of your mission. Of course, you'll want to frame it neatly.

The next thing to be clear about is Purpose. Purpose is distinct from mission in that whilst mission talks about your motivations – *why* you do what you do, purpose talks about what and how you do it.

If in doubt, a great format for a purpose is to fill in the blanks in the following

I/We help (target market) to get from (current problem) to (outcome) in (x) weeks with(out) (obstacle)

For example, I help owners of growing businesses to get from 5 figures to 6+ figures in 12 months without working harder

Other great examples would be "I help people who have been made redundant to get from their old career to a new career in 3 months without dropping their income" or "I help people with a broken tooth get from pain to pain-free in 2 hours, without costing them the earth"

Operating Processes

The second part of Process is the most substantial, understanding the quantity and quality of the existing operating processes in the business, and what level is appropriate in the future.

Some businesses, going into this, have operating processes that are just in someone's head. Whereas for others, there are thick manuals, with absolute, minute detail on every single step. But both of those extremes have problems. Of course, most will lie somewhere in between the two.

Whatever the answer is for your business, you need to start by writing out a list of the high-level processes that are in scope for your change.

This might list things like "bookings", "payment" or "accounts" – the broad areas under which you will categorise your existing processes and procedures.

Under each of these high-level headings, identify who is the key subject matter expert. Wherever possible, try to ensure that this is not the business owner (even if that's you!). It is a common challenge in a growing business that the owner feels like they are the only one who truly understands how everything is done, and how it should be done. By when systemising your business you're going to have to step away from taking that personal control, to make things repeatable and scalable. There may be some areas where you are indeed the only person that understands it, but unless you're a solopreneur, this should not be everything. Systemising your business will be more successful if you can identify clear process owners and get them involved in the changes you need to make, freeing you up to take a bird's eye view of how all of these fit together and to be able to provide challenge and support at arm's length from the hard graft of actually re-writing all of the processes.

Finally, bear in mind that what got you here won't get you there – if you developed all of the existing processes in your business and now have dedicated staff undertaking the work then step back a little and let them shine.

Once you have an owner for each subject area, task them with collating all the material that exists on current processes, and identifying areas where nothing is documented. We're not going to try to fix that yet (that work is part of the execution), but having a clear map of where documentation does or does not exist will be invaluable in deciding how to plan the work. It may also be that the gaps here influence the order of the work later as well. For example, if you have a process that is only in one person's head and you know they are due to retire soon, you might want to start there. Or perhaps the key person you need is on parental leave and due back in 3 months – maybe another area could be prioritised ahead of their return so that they are available.

It's important also to be clear on the right level of documentation. This will vary depending on your industry and the nature of your work. Where you're going to try to get to the end of this is to have essential processes that are documented consistently, to just the right level that an intelligent person with a little bit of thought, can replicate them and get the same outcome.

However, unless you have regulation that requires it or are documenting a safety-critical role, we're not going to try and build a big fat process manual.

This is because when you do that, what you do is you take the thinking out of the work. And once you take the thinking out of the work, it's not very satisfying.

Of course, when we get to the execution stage there'll be some elements of the work where we can literally take all of the thinking out (you'll be looking at those as opportunities where you can use automation to just replicate the task without needing a person in there at all).

However, if you reduce all of the work in your business to a level where it can be done without thinking then working in your business will only appeal to people who don't want to think. It's unlikely that this is going to lead you to have a highly engaged, motivated and creative workforce that will keep your business agile and able to deal with the challenges ahead. More likely you will end up with a disengaged workforce who simply come to work for the money and for whom bending the rules to cope with an unexpected situation is simply not worth the risk to them, even if it leads to a better customer outcome. We have all dealt with companies that have reached this point, where we cannot get any common sense out of them because they just have rules to follow. It is frustrating as a customer and disengaging as an employee. This is not the way to make a business great.

It's an observation that Netflix has made, they have moved away from very detailed procedures manuals, with exactly the observation that they reduce the job to a level that no one had to think about. And therefore no one that liked to think wanted to work for Netflix, and they wanted people with brains who could help them drive their business forward.

At the other end of the spectrum, if it's all in your head, you're probably spending an inordinate amount of time having to tell people how to conduct tasks that you feel they should be able to do themselves. The reason they can't do that themselves is that they don't own the process and the knowledge to work out what the right outcome is - it's all in your head. This means that you're having to do all the thinking for them. The odds are that they are as frustrated with this situation as you are, but without anything documented, no task is repeatable, no outcome is clear and no-one in your business can function without you taking hundreds of micro-decisions.

So there is a balance to be struck... setting out the process is vitally important, it's really important to describe what the correct outcome of the process is, and what the correct steps to achieve it look like. But allow enough latitude individually employees to use their own personal talent and style and how they deliver it because you might just get something better than you possibly imagined by doing that.

Get clear at this stage where the right level of documentation is in your business, and I'd strongly encourage you to plan to produce something just a little lighter than you would feel comfortable doing.

Costs

The final part of Process is costs. You're going to be doing quite a bit of work as you go through the execution phase to try to understand the granular costs of different processes.

However, if you've got any information around costs at a high level to start with, it's really useful to draw that together for a couple of reasons.

Firstly, it's important as we go through this to start to think about where there may be wasted costs in your business. These may result because processes are broken, they are inefficient, they lead to mistakes or they lead to rework. All of those are costs which you want to take out.

A high-level understanding of which processes generate the highest costs at this stage will allow you to better plan where to start on the execution since the scope for cost saving is clearly much higher on processes that generate greater costs.

Secondly, think about what your appetite for costs looks like. Is the main driver for this transformation to reduce the cost base of your business? Knowing this will help you make key decisions if, for example, you come up with a solution that reduces the manual work, but on a cost basis is net neutral because it requires additional technology spending. If your main objective is to reduce costs, then that's not going to be the right outcome for you.

Conversely, if your main objective is to improve customer service as long as costs don't rise, this may be a great solution.

Whether that is a success or a failure as an outcome will depend upon what you are trying to achieve, and where your priorities lie, so it's really important to understand appetites and budgets before going into this. And the nature of technical solutions is that very often there will be an obvious upfront cost. But over the longer period, there will be substantially cheaper than the recurring costs of hiring more people to do the same work.

Of course, whether hiring more people is even a practical solution will depend upon the circumstances and in some businesses, in some situations, it just isn't

6 Technology

The final leg of the pillars is technology. Again, we break this into three sub-components, it's important to think about them. And it's important to get a handle on this before we go in.

Core Tools

So the first one is the core tools, what core tools does your business use? Are you predominantly on Microsoft? Are you predominantly on Google, maybe you're on Apple, maybe on bits of everything? But you need to understand that before we start because it's rarely a cost-effective solution. If you're entirely on one platform to move entirely to another platform. Of course, sometimes it's necessary. But the chances are, it will not be the most cost-effective solution for your business to do that. Equally, if you're spread out around a number of platforms, it can make a lot of sense to consolidate them, it can simplify the administration. It can reduce license costs, it can reduce the amount of maintenance because there's just less complexity in the system. And we often discover, when we work with clients that actually, they've got a lot of the functionality they need within the core tools, but they're not using it because maybe they don't know exists, or because they've already bought something else, so they're paying twice. So that doesn't make a whole lot of sense.

Systems Admin

The second pillar of technology is the systems administration capability you have within your business. And what I mean by that is what level of technical skill Do you have available to you in your business? Around administering computer systems and applications? Now, if you're a very small business, and it's just you really that boils down to how confident or how technophobic are you, around your applications, if you're a larger business, you might want to think about whether you've got one or two people within your business who are maybe a bit more tech-savvy. Those people could become pivotal in both delivering and running, what we're going to build. And it's important to identify that early on because if you don't have those skills and capabilities, you're going to need more external support. It's important that tools are built and configured in the right way and that they're integrated correctly within your business. And if you don't have those skills in house, it will make sense to buy them in. It's a requirement during the build phase. But it also makes sense to think about how you're going to maintain them. Once you go live. There are lots of no-code and low code environments that can be used to do a lot of integrations now, so the technical hurdle to both building and maintaining this stuff is lower than it was. But it's also quite easy to do it wrong. So really challenge yourself to make sure that you've got the right capability to both deliver and maintain the technology that you're going to end up acquiring.

Infrastructure

The final pillar of tech is to think about your infrastructure. By infrastructure, I mean, what is your business running on? I mean, you know, maybe you're already running in the cloud, and that's brilliant. But maybe at the other end of the spectrum, you're running on paper, and there are bits of paper, moving around your organization, maybe it's post-it notes, maybe it's order forms. Somewhere between the two, perhaps you're running it on a PC in the corner of the office. There are different challenges with scenarios, if you're already in the cloud, you are in a better position. But you are also committed to that cloud provider and the services that they support. So there are some considerations there. If you're still on paper, then, on the one hand, you have a lot of opportunities to improve things very easily. But on the other hand, you're starting from a very low technical base, there are lots of very basic services that we will need to develop for you before you can start to get value. In a scenario where you're between those two extremes and running on a local PC, in some respects, you've got the worst of both possible worlds. You've got to do to IT changes there, you've got to move from what you've got today off that and you've got to move on to something new. So you're going to have to unpick existing processes and existing software use and move to something new, which can be more complex. On the other hand, doing so can dramatically reduce the IT risks in your business. It can increase your resilience and can allow your people to work much more flexibly.

7 Systems Thinking

Now you've got a grounding in the theory, it's time to start applying it to your business and removing some of that waste we talked about at the start.

Thinking about some of these problems, some of where this waste occurs, is the kind of thing that I do within my business. To understand the choke points in businesses of various different types, we very often use a technique called Systems Thinking.

"Systems" in this context doesn't mean an IT platform, it means thinking about the whole entity (in this case, the business) in a holistic way and taking a step back and trying to understand overall

What is your business trying to do?

What is it there for?

And what parts have to fit together to make it work?

In some of the traditional ways of thinking about these problems, you think about each piece of the problem individually, and try to optimise that piece (process, piece of software, whatever it might be), to make that bit work really well. You typically do this in isolation, without any thought for how all the bits of the business fit together.

The reason it's a powerful methodology for this sort of stuff is that Systems Thinking steps us back and says actually, what you're trying to do is make everything work together harmoniously. That might mean that every individual piece is only 90%, as good as it could be, but if they all work well together, you'll still get a better result than having each piece of your business being 100% effective but then really terrible at interfacing with others.

When I talk about "pieces of the business", I mean, the component steps like the booking process, the appointment itself, taking payment, your marketing, processes, et cetera. Having all of that joined up holistically, and working together so that each step reinforces the others is vitally important.

As we go through this next section you'll start to see how that works.

Usually, what I find is that there's a core part of the business. So in the case of a therapy business, I expect that what happens in the appointment itself is a piece of the process that you will understand deeply well, because it's the core of your skills, it's the thing that you bring to the world. But often, the rest of the things that need to happen to make that come to life have never been planned through in the same way.

So let's get practical and think about what that means for therapy businesses...

You have the appointment and I'm not going to talk very much about that in this book because that's going to be different for every reader, and also because frankly, you know that way better than I do.

So I'm not going to try and teach you how to how to do that. But, I'm going to try to show you how the whole system fits together around that, and where there may be some opportunities to make life a little bit simpler. I promise that this won't all be high level, theoretical stuff as we go through and you'll start to see how it comes to life, but it is important just that you understand where I'm coming from with this.

The first step is some sort of initial appointment where you assess whether or not you can help this potential client. In this process, we'll call that your Discovery Call since you will be *discovering* whether you can help the client, and they will be *discovering* whether they like to work with you, can afford you etc

After that, you will have a Delivery step, where you deliver your treatment or therapy. That might be a single appointment, but more often it will be a sequence of appointments over a period of time. Again I'm not going to get into the specifics here – each therapy is different and each therapist knows what it takes for them to deliver the desired outcome. Instead, I want to think about the overall process. After each appointment, or perhaps monthly there will also be some sort of payment process to invoice the client as well.

So in process terms, the Deliver and Invoicing steps can be thought of as part of a loop that a client will flow around one or more times repeating the cycle of treatment and payment.

So in summary before the appointment there needs to be some sort of process to book the client in, then you have a treatment appointment where you deliver the therapy. After the appointment, you need to take payment. That's how your business runs booking appointment payment so that's the flow.

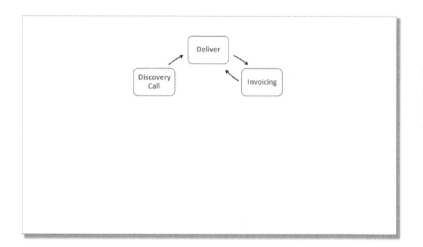

Or is it? Well, I would argue it's not that there's a couple of other steps missing, but ones which are often not considered in anywhere near as much detail.

However, they're equally important if you want to make your business run efficiently so that you can spend your time on that appointment step and not having to do all the other stuff around it. And that's really where we're trying to get to here is that you can spend as much of your time and energy as possible on the thing that you love doing. To do that we want to get to a stage where you've got a self-reinforcing process in your business, that just helps everything to come together, and where each step is helped by the one before it.

Let me explain what I mean by that. Before you get bookings, you have to get clients from somewhere, so some sort of marketing activity has to happen to tell people that you're out there, what you do. Next, you need that activity to bring leads through into your bookings process, so that they can then flow through, book an appointment and become a client. And you may have different levels of sophistication right now around your marketing. You may have some quite advanced stuff going on, or you may not have done very much at all. Marketing in this context can mean a whole load of different things. It could mean Facebook ads, it could mean word of mouth, referrals from happy clients, it could mean traditional print advertisement or email marketing. Whatever form it takes, fundamentally, it's the activity of encouraging people to come and make the booking with you, and it needs to happen before you get any clients into your discovery calls.

But there's another step as well, that I think is hugely overlooked in many types of businesses - and this is very powerful. That step is getting a review and it's powerful for two things.

Firstly, having some sort of a review process and getting a review is very, very powerful in itself, because it is getting you out there. It is the social proof for other potential customers that your business is going to deliver what you say you're going to deliver, you're going to deliver the results that you, you promise.

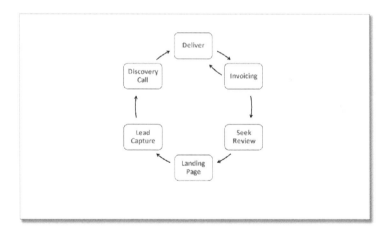

But also, in the way that I've drawn it here, you can see, it's also important for a really simple reason - it joins up the cycle and creates a feedback loop in your business. In

Systems Thinking this is called a Reinforcing feedback loop, and that's important because what that means is you've then got a process that things are moving around. The review process reinforces your marketing, marketing reinforces bookings, which gets you more appointments, which get paid, and you request a review, which feeds into your marketing and the cycle repeats. And so it goes... which means that once you build this, there's an element to which your business becomes more self-sustaining, because, you don't need to be going out the whole time and feeding lots of people into your marketing funnel. Of course, there will be times that you will want to - when you want to take on more clients, and you've got some capacity, but to a greater extent, your business will continue to feed itself in a cycle.

Once you get those sorts of cyclical business processes, they can become really powerful in terms of allowing your business to work for you, rather than you having to work for your business. This, then is your core business loop.

But there are other tasks that need to happen as well.

For a start, simply invoicing a client isn't enough – you'll probably want to actually get paid!

And to leave reviews and make bookings you'll need to interact with review sites and diaries, so these steps need to be added...

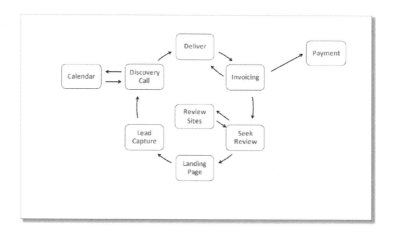

Next, let's think about what happens when you get paid...

Firstly, you need to do your accounts (and I'll talk more about tools for this later in the book)

However, you might want to re-invest some of your income in some advertising. What's that advertising going to do? Well, probably at least two different things. It's going to drive some of your prospective leads directly to your landing page, but where you have cold leads, you'll probably want to drive those to a lead magnet instead.

A lead magnet is simply a piece of value that you give away for free (or occasionally a very small cost) to cold leads (i.e. those who are not yet aware that they have a problem that you can solve – which includes people who know they have the problem but don't know you're the solution, as well as those who may not even realise what the underlying issue is). The objective of this lead magnet is to "warm-up" these cold leads, by starting to educate them.

Indeed you can think of your lead funnel like this…

Clients

Your coldest leads are at the top of the funnel and they are Problem Unaware. They may not even know that they have an issue, and if they do they have not understood properly what it is. Exactly what that means will vary depending on the therapy you're offering but for example, it could include someone who is experiencing several pains but has not yet understood that they are all coming from the same root cause. Clearly, they are aware of the pain, but they have not yet linked up all of these to realise that they have one specific problem. The lead magnet is a short video or download from you that they can watch or read that will help them to realise that these are all just symptoms of an underlying problem that they have... and in so doing, they have become Problem Aware.

Once they are Problem Aware, they may start researching possible solutions. This is where they might hit your website, watch more of your videos or follow you on social media, as they start to understand their problem more and become Solution Aware.

Only once they are aware that there is a solution to their problem, and that solution is your services, are they ready to become a client. If you try to force it sooner, they will not be emotionally and intellectually invested in their recovery and if they do sign up they are quite likely not to show up regularly, put the work in or finish the treatment. I'm sure you'll have seen clients like that in your business – the ones who almost seem like they don't want to get better.

Your discovery call should be bringing in people who are Solution Aware – that is the point at which you're spending time assessing whether or not you can help their specific case, and how you get on with them. The job of your marketing is to take them from a cold Problem Unaware lead to the stage where they are ready to have the Discovery Call.

Advertising will get your lead magnet in front of Problem Unaware people and help them to move to the Problem Aware stage, but it could also target those who are Problem Aware and seek to move them to Solution Aware, by pushing them to your landing pages, where you provide more information on how you solve the problem, they now know they've got. This could be either through retargeting those who have downloaded the lead magnet or by identifying lookalike audiences of people who look and act just like those who have downloaded your lead magnet.

Finally, you may want to target mailings at people who have provided you with their details by signing up for newsletters etc on your landing page but have never become a client. Typically, you will seek to push these people back into your funnel by providing them with information and links back into your landing page ecosystem in the hope that they pick up where they left off, and ultimately decide to book onto a Discovery Call

So once we add all that to the process flow we've got something like this:

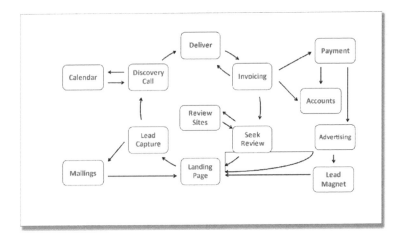

(there's a full-page version of this image at the back of the book)

This is the overall system of your business. I have a good friend who tells me that every time she sees the final stage of this chart it makes her feel anxious because there's so much going on. Really though, there's no need – odds are that *you're already doing all of this.* It's just once to see it drawn out you can start to think about how all these pieces fit together and work better. And if there are steps in here that you're not doing, then *at least now you know!*

It's obviously hugely simplified, there are loads of other things that have to happen underneath these blobs, but at a high level, these steps articulate how your business runs.

Of course, the diagram is also slightly different in different sorts of industries, so if you were in construction, instead of the Discovery Call, you would have some different activity in there like quoting, and your delivery stage might be building a house, but fundamentally, for all businesses, you can distil them down into a cycle that looks broadly like this. Some have got a few extra steps. But for therapy, coaching, tutoring and consulting businesses, these are the key steps.

8 Find The Waste

We then start thinking about some of the problems, you might start to see in each of these steps, and in how the steps interact with each other.

I started the book by talking a bit about the time to schedule, missed appointments, and maybe conflicts with your own personal diary. We've all got things that go on outside of our jobs and our businesses. Maybe you've got kids, or maybe you're caring for relatives, or you've got other activities that rely on your time. And maybe those are not always completely predictable. But you don't necessarily want to manage all of those in your business diary for all to see, and so it makes sense to have a personal diary too. So then you're kind of having to flip between them so that you know whether or not you're free, and if things change, you might have to be calling up clients and rescheduling. These are common problems you may potentially have in the booking stage. You may have others that you can think of too. Start writing these down. Besides the therapeutic value of listing them out, it will help you to tackle them as you get further through the book.

There are a whole bunch of problems that I frequently hear about in the payment stage. Firstly the real practical problems. Payments just failing - someone writes you a cheque and the cheque bounces – less of a problem than it used to be but I still regularly come across therapists who ask for cheques. Or someone says they'll pay on a bank BACS payment, and they just don't so you have to keep chasing them for the payment.

If you take cash, there's the whole issue around cash handling, which is particularly an issue post-COVID when lots of people do not want to handle cash (indeed, this has been the thing that has finally done for cheques as well in many businesses).

So BACS has become a popular choice but if you take your payments by BACS and you're not a limited company with its own bank account, how do you feel about giving out your personal bank details?

A lot of the time I hear people not quite uncomfortable about doing that and having part of my career where I worked for a bank, I can tell you that this is not without good reason, because fraudulent payments can happen if you give out your bank details.

If you take regular payments, then that relies on either the client regularly initiating payment by whatever means or you asking them repeatedly to pay you.

There are also other issues that pop up frequently. Sometimes, particularly in very small businesses, people say that they feel kind of awkward asking people for money for the service provided. That might manifest in terms of delaying asking for payment, or how they set their pricing strategy. Usually, they're not charging as much as they feel they could, because that makes them a bit too uncomfortable to have that conversation with clients and since each payment happens manually, they have to keep having it over and over again.

Finally, we get into more of an accounting issue – you've got to record the payments somewhere, and you may potentially need to issue invoices (obviously, that partly depends on whether you're VAT registered).

If you're VAT registered, then you'll no doubt be aware of the Making Tax Digital (MTD) scheme that requires you to file your VAT returns electronically. If you're not and at the moment, you're managing your payment information, invoicing information on a spreadsheet or a piece of paper, that ultimately will have to come to an end once MTD is rolled out for Corporation Tax because those are not acceptable formats to file tax returns. At that point, you will have to use one of the dedicated tools. You have some time to prepare for this, but certainly, something that is worth having in your mind and thinking about as this will be an issue that needs to be resolved.

The next step of the process is all about Reviews, and I touched again on some of the points on this earlier on.

Actually, a lot of businesses don't get reviews simply because they feel uncomfortable asking. They've given the customer service and been paid and then they don't quite feel that comfortable saying "*oh, by the way, would you would you give me a review?*" Ideally, this is pretty much at the same time as asking for money.

A lot of businesses will ask me whether it even makes a difference?

I'm here to tell you that yes, it does definitely make a difference!

If you can get a good number of reviews on a platform like Google, if you can get your Google My Business with at least 10 ideally 20 to 25, good quality reviews, you will start showing up much more in the searches. Google which means you are easier to find. When people do find you there's a huge body of evidence that shows that they're far more likely to buy from you - some estimates are that new customers are up to 20 times more likely to buy from a business that has a good number of reviews.

Interestingly, it doesn't have to be necessarily straight five star reviews. Most evidence shows that it is most trustworthy to have is 4.7-4.9 on average. This happens because with straight five star reviews, apparently, people think maybe it's a bit manufactured, but we tend to assume that no-one would manufacture a 4-star review!

Therefore it's worth thinking about how to collect them because you should have them.

Another pain point I hear frequently is the risk of accidentally asking twice or more for a review. Imagine you've got someone that comes to you every week, and you then you just keep asking them every week - they're going to get annoyed, and then they might give you a one-star review!

that would be even worse than having no review. That's a concern and a very legitimate one, so you need to have a way of recording who you've already asked.

How will you even know when you get a review? I'm sure you don't wake up in the morning and check your Google listing every single morning. So how do you know when a new review is there? And what if you get a bad review? What if someone's gone on there and put a one-star review on? Sometimes people will do that for reasons that are absolutely not your fault. And you would want a right to reply even though you can't change the review. You would at least want to know what's happened and have the ability to put some sort of comment on there saying that you're sorry, they felt like that, what you did, to make up for whatever the incident was or whatever else you would at least want to provide context.

So it is a source of fear that if you do ask for reviews, then you might trigger someone giving you a bad review. But the reality is that if someone's upset with your service enough to give you a bad review, they're going to go and find your Google listing, give you a bad review or your Facebook listing and give you a bad review - they're not going to wait for you to ask them to do that.

The flip side though, is if they're really happy with your service, they might not give you a good review unless you do ask them. Either because they didn't think to do it, or because they don't understand how important reviews are for small businesses, or maybe just because they forgot.

As you can see, asking is unlikely to significantly change the number of negative reviews you might get from people who have an axe to grind, but it is quite likely to increase the number of positive reviews you get. More positive reviews dilute the power of the odd rogue negative one that might be there and bring your average score up, so you can also see having a large number of legitimate positive reviews as something of an insurance policy against the odd bad one, that might not be your fault.

The last point in the cycle is around marketing. This can cover a multitude of activities.

Who do you market your business to?

What do you say to them?

Where do you do that marketing?

Those are all kind of questions that people say, Oh, actually, I "can't answer these". And so kind of paralysis can set in and end up doing nothing.

Or perhaps you're not clear on who your target client is, in which case potentially all of your marketing activity is wasted effort. This isn't a marketing book and I'm not going to try to solve these here – it is a subject which is well covered with dedicated books. All I will say about this part of the process is that you need to be aware of the pitfalls and make sure you're clear on your messaging and your target audience otherwise no efficiency in the world is going to help you!

Beyond that, look at how you're delivering the marketing, how you're capturing the leads and the mechanics behind delivering the lead magnet to make sure everything is efficient, and that you don't have disconnects in your process, you're not asking for information you don't need, or asking twice for the same information and that you're storing the captured data properly. These are common issues I see in this area and besides inefficiency of this, you may also be in breach of GDPR (which is incorporated into UK law as the Data Protection Act 2018) or other regulations if you are holding inaccurate data, holding it in an unsecured manner and don't have consent to hold and use it. Bear in mind that paper records are in scope for this legislation so you can't side step the legal obligations by simply recoding contact details in an address book on paper. In fact, doing so presents far greater risks in complying with the requirements for security and being able to evidence timely removal of information, than an electronic record ever would.

That's a quick summary sort of the problems that we usually see therapy businesses identify when they go through this approach. I'm sure you will identify with some of them, and will also have some of your own. The important thing however is that once you've got the process documented and have brainstormed all the problems and waste in each step, and between them, then you can start solving some of this.

9 Fix My Business

You now understand all the places where you waste time in your business - so let's start solving it. This is the Execution phase.

In the sections that follow, I'll give you specific practical advice about which tools you can use in each stage of your therapy business and the trade-offs between them. However, I'd reiterate that software is constantly changing and whilst these recommendations are valid at the time of writing (April 2021), you should validate that they hold true before committing to any specific product.

Firstly, I'm going to suggest a fundamental change in your process. Some of you reading this may be completely fine with this or be doing it already, and other people may absolutely feel this is unacceptable, but here goes...

Stop asking for payment after you've delivered your services. Ask them to pay, in full, when they book.

Doing this simultaneously solves a few issues.

Firstly, you get paid earlier in the process, which is great for cash flow. Secondly, your no-show rate will drop dramatically, because people who have paid will make more effort to show up. Thirdly even if they don't show up, you've already been paid for the time, so it's just a bonus opportunity to work on your business, take a break, or whatever. Finally, you remove any sort of process around chasing for late payments, and as a bonus, you break the timing link between payment and review.

If you aren't convinced despite all of this, I would gently challenge you to just try it, even if at first you think that will never work - and look at the results objectively.

I often hear that there's no way a therapist could switch around the payment and appointment order and ask people to pay before they've had their appointment.

Well, try it - because, most goods that we buy, you pay before you use them. Packaging up your services into a product makes this far easier to do. You're selling an outcome, not your time and if people know what they're going to get, and you ask them to pay they will generally be fine with doing that (perhaps you need to give them comfort by saying, if you put in the work and you're still not happy, you'll get a money-back guarantee).

As I say, if someone has paid you, the no show rate will go through the floor, because they've already paid out for that point they have committed to you. It's in their head, they feel that they want to be there. Whereas if you're collecting the payment at the time of the appointment, and they choose to cancel the day before the appointment at that point, they haven't made any commitment financially and therefore probably emotionally to you. So it's a good strategy for reducing no shows, and although I've had some quite strong reactions when I've posed this to groups, some of the people who strongly pushed back when I suggested it went away, tried it came back and said "*You know what, it turns out that it works fine. None of our clients are complaining, they're all fine with it, they get it*".

Even if you just try it with one or two clients, maybe you've got some repeat offenders who you always have to chase for payment, that's probably a great place to begin.

Having made that switch, the next thing to think about is how all the bits of this problem fit together.

So let's start thinking about each of these steps and what can do inside each one - but through the lens of how it fits into the overall system, the overall process.

10 Appointment Booking

We talked a bit about all of the issues with booking already. There is a really simple solution here, which is to put your diary system online, make it directly available to clients. Nearly all of the issues we surfaced with Booking can be quickly solved with this change.

It will remove the time spent booking clients in, it will reduce no-shows and it will also allow you to control which periods of the week you use for different types of appointments.

For example, you might decide that you see brand new clients on a Tuesday morning, that you do discovery calls on a Thursday afternoon, or that you only do follow-ups on a Monday. All of these things can be easily configured with an online diary, and blocking your time like this will enable you to be focused on the right type of work at the time in the week that works best for you.

The first thing that people freak out about when I talk about putting their diary online is client confidentiality. Don't worry about this. The systems I recommend here will all mask your actual diary from anyone seeking to book into it – they will simply be offered slots when you are free, that align to whatever rules you've built into the system. They won't get any information on what you're spending the rest of the week doing, whether that's other client work, working on your business, or indeed sitting on a beach!

This avoids any risk of any sort of data security / GDPR issues you would have with just publishing your diary for all to see, but it also keeps your personal privacy under control.

You can hook up your business diary (to put bookings in) and also have these tools check your personal diary for conflicts (maybe you use a personal diary to track family appointments such as school, dentist etc which you share with other family members, or just don't want to put into your business diary)

I already talked about how you can reduce the cancellations by taking payment upfront. With a diary booking system, you can do that by taking electronic payment as part of the booking process for some or all of your meetings.

You can automatically issue any forms that need to be filled in before the appointment, any instructions required (particularly helpful for initial appointments) and you can further reduce no-shows by automatically issuing reminders, with any relevant information 24 hours (or whatever time you consider appropriate) before the appointment.

So by the time they come in for the appointment, you've already got all of that information completed, which means you don't have to potentially sit them in a waiting room or wherever else and ask them to fill out a paper form because they've done it will go ahead of time

Think about how much work that could save you. All of the material you'd normally send to a client before their appointment can be automated, questionnaires required to feed into discovery calls can be automated, and you can issue automated follow-up emails with further information and (jumping ahead slightly) a link to leave a review.

With some smart mailbox rules, you can also have responses to any forms automatically filtered and filed, so that all you have to do on the day of the appointment is to open up the document and read it.

Many therapists, and other professionals, have transitioned some or all of their work to video calls during 2020 and if any of your appointments work like this you'll be pleased to know that you can integrate the booking systems with the most common video platforms to allow you to have the link automatically set up as well.

All of this can all happen completely on the clients time, it could be 3:00 am for them and they could suddenly think "*I really want to get this booked in*". They could go online, find a slot in your diary, book it and pay and receive all the materials they need to confirm the appointment. You would get up the next morning to find it's already in your diary for the right date, payment is already on the way and forms have been returned. All requiring no work from you to negotiate the time, no work from you to process the payment or anything else you can see right there booked in and already paid.

That's an immediately huge time saver for a lot of businesses, but it's also a great piece of customer service. We're all conditioned to use our smartphones to just get or book what we want, when we think of it, and if your business can support that then you're immediately working on your client's schedule and making it easy for them to get booked in, and equally importantly, for them to get the confirmation that it's been done. They can then stop thinking about it until the date of the appointment, rather than having to track it as an "open" item in their head until they hear back from you to confirm.

You might think that the number of times people want to book at weird hours is minimal, but once you implement this you may be surprised. I had one therapist report to me that she took 15 new client bookings on the afternoon of Christmas Day (her busiest single day for new clients ever), and I myself have taken bookings for consulting work at 4 am, on public holidays, and frequently on weekends – all times that I'd rather not be having to monitor my email! There's something that feels magical about taking a day off, and coming back the next day to find that people have booked and paid you, whilst you were busy relaxing!

Tools I recommend for calendar-booking are Calendly, Acuity or x.ai. The core functionality of each is similar, but there are some specific features that some have and others don't. Beyond that, it is largely personal preference on the look and feel of the tools and the price point that gives you the features that matter most to you. For example, at the time of writing, if you want to be able to use SMS reminders then Calendly will offer it at a lower price plan than Acuity, and x.ai doesn't offer it at all. On the other hand, x.ai offers the ability to simply cc it on a normal email conversation, as you might a PA and it will attempt to parse the email, understand what you're looking for and book it, which can lead to a more personal experience than the other platforms offer.

We'll look at each in turn, but bear in mind that all software platforms are in an arms race of sorts and features that prove popular on one platform can be rapidly copied onto another, so whilst this summary is accurate at the time of writing (April 2021), you should check the current feature set and pricing before making a selection

Calendly

Calendly is one of the most popular tools, with over 8 million users worldwide. As one of the more established options and fully focussed on providing you with an online booking tool, the system is simple to use but has powerful options.

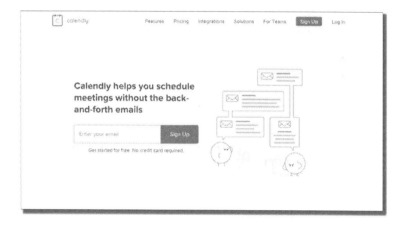

Calendly offers the ability to share a booking link via email, directing users to your booking page, or you can embed your diary on your website. On the paid plan, Calendly branding is removed and you can make it look well integrated (for an example see mine: https://cobaltbeach.com/free-initial-consultation)

One nice feature is the ability to generate a "one time link" which you can send to someone to book just a single instance of an appointment. It cannot be reused, meaning it is ideal for any sort of new client welcome meeting with a different fee from the normal appointment.

And talking of fees, you can set up payment at the time of booking, by linking to Stripe or PayPal. Reminders can be issued by email, or from the standard plan upwards, by SMS

Calendly supports group bookings (useful if you run classes) as well as features such as padding, which ensure that people can't book you without leaving you a break before or after (or both)

Calendly is generally considered the simplest tool to start using, although there are advanced options available using its automation and workflow options which will allow you to determine sequences of follow-up messages to be sent before and/or after the meeting.

Acuity Scheduling

Acuity Scheduling is another strong option. Produced by Squarespace (who you may know from the website builder) it also has a simple yet powerful interface and a strong feature set.

It too offers the ability to connect to all main diary providers, allows embedding of your calendar in a webpage or ability to access a booking page via a sharable link. Again, different meeting types and schedules are accommodated as are paid and group bookings.

One area where it falls down against Calendly is if you use Microsoft Teams as your main video conferencing tool. Whilst it is possible to connect Acuity to Teams, you'll need to build a connector in a third-party tool such as Zapier (potentially at extra cost, depending on your existing Zapier plan).

Uniquely among these tools, it offers an affiliate marketing scheme, so if you want to make a little extra cash by convincing your friends to use it, that is an option too!

SMS reminders are available, but you'll need to upgrade beyond the standard plan to use them ($23 per month at the time of writing). General-purpose workflow is not part of the tool and you'll need to build this in another tool such as Zapier.

x.ai

x.ai has taken a different approach to meeting scheduling, although it has grown to incorporate a number of similar features. Consider using this tool if you want a system that feels more like a human PA doing the booking, but can live without certain features, such as SMS reminders.

x.ai uniquely provides the ability for you to copy in your "AI Assistant" on an email and request a meeting is set up. The artificial intelligence will parse the email and attempt to set up the meeting as requested. The level of success will be dictated by how clearly you make your request, but increases over time as the system trains itself on your writing style. Recipients will then receive a follow-up email from the system requesting times (which have been pre-vetted against your diary) and will continue to correspond with them until all participants have chosen a time and the meeting is booked.

Whilst x.ai does offer a bookings page and sharable link, the simple to use email process is its real strength. The bookings page is less configurable than with either Acuity or Calendly, although like both of those tools it can support multiple meeting types, including paid appointments (via Stripe)

The main gripe x.ai solves is that simply sending someone a link via a traditional tool can feel impersonal, and like you are offloading the work onto them, as well as requiring them to break out of a naturally flowing email conversation to use another tool, which risks losing engagement. By embedding the scheduling request directly in the email but concierging the whole service, your customer gets a better experience and drop out rates are lower.

Personally, I love this tool and I use it alongside Calendly (which is my tool of choice for bookings via my website), for those times where an email feels more natural than sending a self-service link. However, most people will not want to use multiple tools, and the x.ai platform does take a bit more work to understand.

Microsoft Bookings

However, if you're already using Microsoft 365 and have determined that for whatever reason you don't want to take online payment then you should take a look at Microsoft Bookings – it's already included in your Microsoft 365 subscription and does everything you'll need, except for connecting to an online payment gateway.

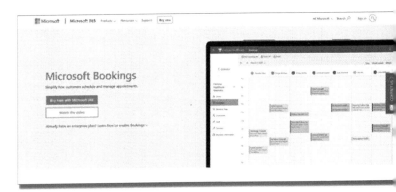

The first thing to note is that if you're not using Microsoft then you may as well skip this section right now. It only integrates with your Outlook diary and is only available as part of the Microsoft 365 bundle. That said, for less than the price of most of the other tools on the list you get ALL of Microsoft 365 including Bookings, but also Word, Excel, Outlook, PowerPoint and around 20 other tools so if you're not strongly tied to another platform then it's well worth considering the benefits case for ditching everything else and moving to Microsoft.

The tool itself provides a booking page, which can be embedded on a website. Look and feel configuration options are much improved from earlier versions, but not quite as flexible as Acuity or Calendly but you should be able to roughly match the rest of your site.

Integration with Teams is of course excellent, but if you use another video platform such as Zoom or Google Meet, you'll have to rely on an external integration via Zapier to generate the links, which is both extra cost and complexity. SMS reminders are also not available.

Other Tools

There are several other tools available and this is a growing market. One that is well worth considering for therapists is an integrated solution such as Cliniko, which not only provides the scheduling capabilities outlined above but also the ability to store client records as well. If you're keen to go fully digital then Cliniko is an excellent option. However, if you're not ready for such a jump yet, be aware that there is a cost for all these extra features, and if you're only going to use it as a scheduling platform then it is an expensive choice.

Cliniko comes into its' own when you use it to run your whole practice. It can manage client records, provides a secure video platform, incorporates accounting functionality such as invoicing and allows you to use marketing tools like SMS messages to your clients.

If you're ready to do all of this then it's a great choice and will save you money against doing all of this on different platforms.

Other platforms that provide similar functionality include Power Diary, Youcanbook.me and Setmore, but others are being developed all the time.

11 Payments

We then move on and think about the payment step. Hopefully, you're already convinced that taking payment at the time of booking is the way ahead, but whenever in your process you take the payment, some issues arise around how you take that payment.

Again, solving these in isolation is better than not solving them, but it's so much more powerful to combine solutions and provide a seamless experience to your client.

What do I mean by that?

Well if you're implementing an online booking system but you currently take payments by BACS (and to be clear, that's just the practice of giving out your sort code and account number so that people can make a payment) then I would urge you to think again.

If you take payment at the time of booking via a credit card, you will be able to ensure that the payment is received before the booking is even completed and put in the diary. All of this will happen automatically, saving you time.

Now I hear you raise the objection that doing this via a platform like Stripe costs you 1.4% transaction fee whereas doing it via BACS doesn't, but here's the thing... you're almost certainly costing yourself more than 1.4% in the amount of time it takes to chase payments. Maybe you have some late payers who need lots of reminding? And sometimes, you can even lose clients over this. Receiving 98.6% of something is worth a lot more than receiving 100% of nothing and when we run the numbers I seldom see a therapist who is not better off by simply paying the 1.4% transaction fee to know that the payment is received before the appointment happens and that no chasing is required.

From a security perspective, it is also massively more sensible than publishing your bank details for all to see, much harder for payments to go astray, and much more trackable.

As with so much of the advice in this book, you *can* simply keep doing things the free, manual, hard way. But a small investment here releases your time, which is much more valuable.

It is also a better client experience as well. Instead of having to book and then go into their internet banking and type in your details to make the payment, they are simply taken through a screen that requests their credit/debit card details as part of the booking process and never need to leave your process, meaning it is quicker, easier and they are more likely to complete it.

In terms of issues that can arise with payments, the biggest is what to do about a customer who fails to pay, The beauty of this solution is that if the payment is going to fail, it will fail when the client tries to pay on their card, at the time of booking. They won't even complete the booking process if they haven't been able to pay and so that problem just literally just goes away.

Cash handling and banking also go away as issues, because you're taking payment online.

For regular customers, you can even set those payment gateways up to take a regular payment, allowing you to take a monthly payment if you've got a subscription plan similar.

You don't even need to have a face to face or telephone discussion with your client because it's just part of the booking process. They go on, they choose the slot, the payment window comes up, they put in their details, press OK takes the payment and books the appointment it sends them an email to confirm and they're paid.

So all that manual process just goes away, but better yet, it also creates electronic records of the payments. Those can be used to issue invoices (if you're a business that needs to invoice), and they can also feed directly into an accounting system.

12 Accounts

Accounts is an area that a lot of business owners find a chore. Often I find that therapists are doing their accounts on Excel or Google Sheets. Occasionally I find they're not even doing that.

Using a spreadsheet package you already have to do your accounts can seem like an attractive idea, but it's another example where you're trading time for money and doing it this way is more expensive in the long run.

A dedicated accounting package is not an expensive outlay and will allow you to do a number of tasks simply and smoothly.

Firstly you can track all of your income and expenses, produce invoices and record bills. These records are essential for running any business, and of course, you need them for your tax returns.

However, it doesn't end there. An accounting package will allow you to integrate with your bank account, with your Stripe and/or PayPal – which means that you can reconcile these transactions directly to what's happening in your bank account and get a view of your cash flow. Once set up correctly you'll be able to see a predicted cash flow showing what bills are due and what invoices you have outstanding – critical information for any business.

You will be able to automatically create your tax and VAT returns within the software, which will save a great deal of time, and with the right integrations, you'll be able to import bills simply by emailing them to the right address and having them scanned in. All of this dramatically reduces the amount of busy-work involved in your accounting, meaning that you can use time on your finances to look at what's happening and actually understand the financial status of your business, rather than just entering data into a spreadsheet.

If you want deeper analysis, all of these packages provide some onboard capability, or you can export to Excel for more advanced analysis if that's something you want to do.

By linking your payment gateway to both your booking system and your accounting platform you can have a setup where your clients book and pay, an invoice is automatically generated and sent, and the sale is recorded in your accounts for your tax return – all without you having to touch anything.

Similarly, your bills can be set up so that on receipt a mailbox rule automatically forwards them directly into your bill management system, which scans them and loads them into your accounting system.

All that leaves you to do is to reconcile these transactions to your bank statement (which should be a quick and simple task at this point) and you have all the data you need to stay on top of your Profit & Loss, your cash flow and do your tax returns, along with all of the evidence you require to prove those things.

In my experience, Xero is the best accounting platform for integrations, followed by QuickBooks. Xero comes packaged with a bill management system called Hubdoc at no extra cost (if you opt for QuickBooks then you can still use this but you'll need to pay extra) and starts at a very low monthly cost.

Rather than having to manually enter information into a spreadsheet where you might make typing the wrong day or the wrong amount and the wrong name or all those other things that might go wrong might not discover until you get to the end of your tax year your bank accounts will sync every few hours, meaning that if anything is wrong, you'll spot it quickly, whilst it's still in your memory and that makes it far easier to fix any issues.

If you have an accountant or bookkeeper you can grant them special access at no extra cost so that they can do your tax returns etc

13 Written Records

Depending on the type of therapy that you offer, the level of client records you hold may vary dramatically. For example, for physiotherapists, there may be a need to record pain points on body images, whereas for therapists working in other disciplines notes might be very different.

Whatever form of client notes you hold, these can be collated electronically. If you like to handwrite your notes during the session then you might want to consider a tablet with a stylus to allow to you write directly to a screen, and capturing an image of this into your records.

Platforms like Cliniko or Power Diary will allow you to capture your client records before, during or after a session, and keep them stored with other materials for this client, which can dramatically save time between appointments, and facilitate easier sharing of notes with the client or between therapists at a shared practice.

I'm not going to go deeply into it here, but I will just make a quick point about an objection I've heard raised many times before. Some therapists will say

"I don't have electronic records, because I'm worried about GDPR".

Unfortunately, GDPR (incorporated into UK law as Data Protection Act 2018) applies just as much to paper records as it does to electronic records. If you are of the mindset that GDPR compliance makes it better to stay with paper then I have bad news for you. Which is that you are already in scope for GDPR and in fact, it's a lot harder to prove you're compliant if your records are on paper than if they're electronic.

This is because they're on paper, you can't prove who has read them or who has not. If they're electronically held then with many systems you can tell who's accessed them, you can also demonstrate that you are meeting the requirement to adequately secure them and you can be certain you can comply with any Data Subject Access Request (DSAR) by supplying all of them. On paper, you have no audit trail, cannot prove that they have been kept adequately secured at all times and cannot be certain you haven't missed, dropped or misfiled a page before releasing copies of the information under a DSAR.

Voice Transcription

If you conduct most of your consultations by video (or indeed, if you like to dictate yourself notes, which you then type up later) I have another substantial time-saving opportunity for you.

Automated transcription services have come a long way in the last couple of years. And whilst until recently they were unreliable, and expensive and typically required a substantial amount of your time afterwards to clean up the recording, there are, now, artificial intelligence solutions. These allow you to transcribe almost any voice notes you may have and which over time will learn your voice, ensuring better match rates, the more you speak to them.

Even the fastest typist, maybe hitting 100 words per minute is still typing somewhat slower than normal human speaking speed. An average English speaker will speak around 150 words per minute in normal conversation. Although when experienced, dictating notes that typically be done at anything up to 180 words per minute. Of course, many people are unable to dictate that fast when they first start - it is a learned skill, and often it is quite difficult to remember what you wanted to say next.

However, voice transcription is incredibly powerful when it's used to transcribe a normal conversation between a therapist and their client. During the flow of that conversation, all sorts of useful information that you may need to record in the notes will be discussed. It will be discussed in a normal, conversational, way and you will have a written copy of what your clients said, in their own words.

Of course, it's essential that you get your clients permission for audio or visual recording before starting, and of course, you must treat the recording in accordance with GDPR rules. However, those hurdles are relatively easy to overcome. In fact, we all experience this every day. Every time you phone through to a call centre you're undoubtedly used to hearing the message about calls may be recorded for training purposes, and it's the same thing. Indeed for some therapists, recording, and being able to further analyse your calls will be a form of ongoing training and will allow them to perhaps understand where conversations, did not go in the direction that they had expected, which might allow them to better understand and anticipate a client's needs and future.

Fundamentally, however you use it, it is an enormous time-saver. It gives you the ability to record the conversation, walk out of the consultation, upload it to machine transcription service, go and get on with your next consultation and come back and find that an hour's worth of text has already been transcribed and maybe just needs a little bit of cleaning up. Compare that with a process where you've written extensive, extensive notes over the hour, and, potentially, then have to spend another hour or so, going through them and typing them up.

Of course, different therapies will require different levels of notes, some may be fairly cursory, some may be largely visual in nature (which obviously do not lend themselves well to voice transcription), but others the verbal element may be substantial and the main area of focus. In these cases, it may be important to capture large blocks of what the client says in their own words, to better support them.

With that in mind, one of the services that it is well worth looking into is otter.ai, or there is also a similar service called fireflies.ai. Both of these are cloud-based, artificial intelligence-powered, transcription services.

In my business, I use otter.ai extensively. I will frequently (with clients agreement of course) record a consultation. I will then feed the results of that into Otter and allow it to transcribe it, which makes it very easy for me to then search for specific areas they may have talked about. This is extremely useful for me when I'm doing something like a business process map and I know that we talked about some parts of their process where they had a specific problem but

I want to hear exactly what they said to make sure that I have correctly understood the detail of it before doing some research on how to support them.

However, it also has uses far beyond that. In your marketing materials for example. You may already be recording videos as part of your marketing (and indeed if you're not, I would say, strongly that you should be!) and perhaps you're presenting webinars. Maybe you're doing talks to networking groups. Whichever those things you're doing if you can get hold of the video or audio recordings you can upload them into a tool like Otter and have them transcribed and immediately, you have a large body of text that is in a very suitable format to form the backbone of your next blog post.

Through this mechanism, you can multipurpose material. You may do a talk to a networking group for 10 minutes, which is useful to those in the room. To get wider value, you may video that talk, and upload it to your YouTube channel - that's fantastic and will be useful for others in the future! You may extract some snippets of that video and use them in your social media, and with a service like this, you can also take the transcription and use it in your blog (indeed if you transcribed, several hours worth of video then you may even find that you've got the basis of a book). Suddenly, what you have is a whole host of marketing assets produced from one 10 minute experience, and the beauty of it is that all of them are in your own words, and what you say in all the different media that you talk to your potential clients with is completely aligned.

Another use is, he can also generate subtitles for your videos with voice transcription, which makes them more accessible, both for those who require subtitles and when played on social media, where many people will watch them with the sound turned off.

So I'm a big fan of voice transcription services and I use them extensively. Most months, transcribe over 10 hours of text this way, which is the equivalent of 90,000 words! Indeed, much of this book has been dictated to the mobile app of otter.ai, as a means to write it for faster than I could type it (and I should say that with over 25 years in IT, my typing speed may not be 100 words a minute, but it's pretty quick!)

Therefore I would urge you to look at voice transcription services as a potential tool that can be used to save time in your business. Think about where you're typing up or writing up notes, and think about whether it would be appropriate, and practical to record them instead. If you can record directly to the mobile app, or if you're using a video platform such as Zoom, you can do real-time transcription.

That will allow you to be generating the written notes in real-time, alongside the conversation, which also frees you up as a therapist to spend your time focused and concentrating on listening to your client, rather than half-listening, half writing, trying to maintain eye contact, trying to check what you've written, turning the page, and generally, not giving anything 100% of your attention.

The transcriptions themselves are also bonded to a timestamped audio file, so as you read the transcription, you can also hear what was said at the time it was said, which will also allow you to pick up on things like tone of voice, that may be important for some therapists.

If you're dictating your own notes, you can talk at whatever speed you're comfortable talking (you can take as long a pause as you need to, to gather your thoughts... had I not told you, you probably would not have realised that I paused for 30 seconds during that last sentence!). but over time you will find that your natural pace increases.

The tools aren't perfect yet, but they are improving all the time. They will learn your voice, and they will learn the most common words that you say, and because of that, they will improve simply through use.

The very competitively priced £10 a month plan will get you ten hours a month of transcription, which is quite a lot and you can add more time if you need it. Compare that to human transcription that can often run to $1 per minute and you can start to see that this is a pretty attractive solution.

14 Reviews

Earlier, we talked about things that happened after the appointment and I touched on the subject of reviews. In terms of asking for reviews, what if you had a tool that after the appointment automatically put your clients into a structured process that would seek to gain a review?

Well such tools exist, and they use similar techniques to the way we market to leads to bring them into your business, but instead of seeking to warm leads up for a sale, they seek to gain a review.

These tools have a funnel into which clients are placed after their appointment which will then send them a message and say something like "I, hope you had a great appointment today. If you did, would you mind leaving me a review?"

And then if maybe after a week, if no review has been left it will follow-up with another one, which perhaps emphasises that it really makes a difference to get these recommendations. And maybe one final one a month to anyone who still hasn't left a review. The tools are smart enough to know if they've already emailed someone in the last six months (say) and not repeat the process.

Another thing to do is to monitor those reviews. Of course, your reviews might go on Google, they might go on Facebook, they might go on various other places (Google and Facebook are the two key ones for therapists). Doing this manually is quite tedious but there are tools that will do this for you. They can alert you to a poor review so that you can respond quickly and positively to it, and they can alert you to a great review, which you would want to share.

When you get a good review, it could immediately publish that to your social media, which feeds back into your marketing processes. A timely five-star review is great marketing.

If you haven't got that sort of system, then you're most like either not asking for and monitoring reviews, in which case you're missing a huge marketing opportunity, or you are creating a piece of completely unnecessary manual work for yourself.

There are different ways of implementing this, depending on the other tools you use. If you use a CRM system to track your client details, and it has automation functionality that you are already using for your marketing funnel, that this is a great place to build your review funnel as well. Tools like Active Campaign are ideal for this as you can set up a review funnel alongside your marketing ones and you may use the same customer list to drive both.

If you're looking for the ability to monitor reviews and share great ones to social media then Embed Social or Nicejob are worth a look. My personal favourite is Nicejob because it offers a great choice of ways to use reviews, from website badges and pop-ups through to automated posting on the main social networks immediately you receive a good review. On the paid plans it also includes the best review funnel I've seen, but unfortunately, that comes with a price tag to match and is therefore unlikely to be a good investment for a small therapy business. That said, it has good functionality on the free plan to help you to capitalise on your good reviews.

You'll no doubt have seen some of this functionality from a customer perspective as you've travelled the web. One of the best-known services for this is Trustpilot, and I'm often asked why I don't recommend it. The simple answer here is just cost. Similarly to CRM tools like Salesforce, it is a brilliant tool, but it is designed for big businesses and has a price tag to match. For a small business, it's far too expensive and you'll never need many of the features that give rise to that price tag anyway.

Related to reviews, I've already talked a bit about Google My Business (GMB). If you haven't got your GMB page claimed, make sure you get a Google My Business account set up right away.

You can do this by going to the Google homepage, logging in and the little grid of dots in the top right-hand corner, if you click on that, you'll see there's an option that says My Business. Click on that and go through and help you find your business and claim it. You can fill in lots of information around when you're open, where you are and websites etc and this will become the detail that Google will show in the sidebar whenever someone looks up your business, as well as being used in Google Maps and elsewhere. So if you haven't done that, that is hugely powerful in terms of getting you found on Google so do it right away.

The other platform that is becoming increasingly important is the Bing equivalent because Microsoft is pushing out the Edge browser more and more aggressively to anyone on Windows 10 (which is a lot of users). I think a fair proportion of people over few updates are going to find that by default they are now using Edge rather than Chrome as their browser. Edge by default uses Bing rather than Google, so this is part of a deliberate strategy to drive search there. The Bing equivalent to GMB is called Bing Places for Business. Again, you access it from the front page of Bing with a similar process to add your business details. In fact, they have added a feature where you can simply sync it to your Google My Business listing, so you only have to maintain one of them, which is very helpful.

15 Marketing

Given that it happens at the start of the business process, you may wonder why I've left it until this point to talk about marketing. The main reason is that when thinking about this, you're going to want to take into account elements from every other step because done right the systems here should simplify everything else, and done wrong they will complicate it.

I'm not suggesting that you implement changes to the marketing process last. But I am suggesting that you make sure you understand all the places where this will touch before doing it.

Why is this so far-reaching? Well for a start, I would advocate that every business should have some form of Customer Relationship Management (CRM) system. Your CRM is your database of all your clients, all your leads and all your contacts. It is the modern-day equivalent of index cards, phone book and mailing list.

Your CRM might be built into whatever you already use – if you have decided to invest in a practice management system such as Cliniko then at least your existing clients will be within there.

However, your other systems may only capture clients, rather than leads, or may not have the functionality you'll want and for that reason, a CRM might be something that you invest in. Invest may have the wrong implications because there are some good free plans around but choosing the one that works for you is an investment of time at least, which you will need to make.

When choosing the right CRM you'll need to consider

- Whether it integrates with the other tools you use
- Whether you can configure it to match your sales process
- Whether it can capture everything you need
- Whether it can support all of your marketing activities

This is a lot for a single tool, and most likely this is an area where you will need to make trade-offs. Let's take these points in turn and consider why they matter, and what to think about.

Integration

Integration between your systems is at the heart of getting the right automation in place in your business. Some tools integrate natively with each other, or in some areas, one tool can do multiple jobs (sidestepping the issue completely). However, what you'll want to avoid at all costs is a system that is closed, and requires you to rekey information to get it elsewhere. Rekeying is just a straight-up waste of time. Any system that doesn't allow you to automatically read in records created elsewhere, or share its records with other systems is following an outdated view of the world, and you should walk away from it. With the widespread use of cloud-based software services, this way of thinking is simply not something you need to entertain.

Of course, it is unreasonable to expect every piece of software to natively work with every other, across every industry, geography, language and so on – the number of combinations would be astronomical! Fortunately therefore there's a class of integration tools you can use to make that happen. Middleware tools such as Zapier, Automate.io and

Autto are designed to provide connectors that can bridge this gap. As long as your chosen package can integrate with one of them, then you'll be able to automate your connections.

Zapier is the most well known and has the greatest number of integrations (about 2000 at the time of writing), and unless there's a specific reason to use another, this is the tool I recommend. Even if your chosen CRM system does not natively support Zapier, a skilled developer will be able to create you an integration as long as the tools at both ends have some sort of Application Program Interface (API), which just about every modern software supports. APIs and middleware tools allow you to get creative about how things happen in your business... do you want to plant a tree every time you get a review? You can do that! (and indeed my business does, using a custom-built connector between Google and the carbon offset organization Tree Nation)

Configuration
Configuration of the sales process is a key feature in being able to match the journey taken by a lead to becoming a client, with the data you hold about them.

IT stands to reason therefore that if you can't properly configure the CRM to match your business, you'll end up having to match your business process to the CRM.

In some industries, this is not a big deal, but for therapists, the process of helping a client to become Solution Aware is a sensitive one and needs to be done without any sort of a "sales" overlay. Therefore any CRM that forces your thinking into a sales pipeline that's all about deal size and closing dates is going to be a terrible fit for your business.

Pretty much all CRM systems allow customisation of the pipeline but be aware that for many it is a paid feature only, so if you're hoping to get by with a free product here, you may need to consider this.

Data Scope

Another feature that might only be available on paid plans, or in some cases may not be available at all, is the ability to tailor the information you capture and to add custom fields.

Generally, all of the key contact fields you could want (name, email, phone, address etc) are the core of the CRM and will be well served.

However, you may need to track a key date such as the date an injury occurred so that you can follow up after a certain time period, or whether the client is left or right-handed, or has allergies. If you need to do these things then you'll probably need to create custom fields to hold this information, in which case investigate whether you can do this (and how many) before making a selection.

You may also find that by using a practice management platform you need to do a lot less customisation (saving set up time) since the platform is already geared to therapy and clinic environments and may have some or all of your needs built-in as standard, whereas a more general-purpose CRM will not.

Activity Scope

The final point to consider is how much of your activity the tool can support.

Some CRM tools (such as Hubspot) have plug-ins that can automatically file all of your email correspondence against the contact. This can be a huge time-saver if email is your major form of communication.

Others such as Mailchimp, are much more heavily focused on supporting your email marketing and mailing list. These provide great features for mailings and ensuring GDPR compliance, but are weaker on the general tracking of contacts.

Active Campaign sits somewhere between these two in terms of capability, with great funnels and mailing capability, but less contact tracking than Hubspot and slightly fewer integrations than Mailchimp. Nonetheless, it has one of the best automation offerings on the free and lower-tier paid plans, and area where Hubspot can quickly become expensive.

Practice management packages often allow you to bulk email existing clients and manage their data well. But these may lack the ability to track leads and bring them through your onboarding funnel.

Finally, there are "business in a box" solutions like Zoho One and Dubsado, which seek to provide a whole host of tools including CRM, mailing lists and others such as electronic contracts, landing pages, and social media scheduling all under one package. Whilst these can be great value for money, they may also be complex to configure, and expensive when you scale your business up since licencing is per user.

So you can see that there are a number of trade-offs to make here. I rarely find a business where one application completely meets all of their needs.

However, there is good news – using integration middleware like Zapier it is fairly simple to mix and match tools, as long as you are very clear on which you are using where and which is the master system for each type of record.

Landing Pages

The other thing a good CRM system can potentially do is to provide you with landing pages. These are really simple one-page websites that you can drive people to for specific topics as part of your funnel.

You may wonder why you'd want to do this instead of driving them directly to your website, but there's a massive amount of research that shows that landing pages are more effective at converting. This is because they are far simpler, and when a cold lead who knows nothing about you hits your site, it is usually because they have asked a very specific question and are looking for a simple answer. Within 6-8 seconds they will assess whether the page they have landed on answers their query, and leave if it does not.

In this instance, less is definitely more. They do not care about how long you've been practising, what certificates you hold, or anything else – they simply want to know if you can answer their question. The more information that is on the site, the more chance that they will not know that before the 6-8 second attention window closes and will just move on.

A well-designed landing page is intended to do a single job, cleanly and efficiently – get them to hang about long enough, and then convince them effectively enough that you can help their very specific problem, that they chose to leave their details. It may do this on-page, or by delivering a lead magnet such as a PDF or video via email, once they provide it, but that should be all it does. Links to your main website should of course be provided, but they should firmly take a back seat to the headline and content on these pages.

Tools like Mailchimp and Active Campaign are great places to build an array of single page landing pages for this purpose, and with a little knowledge, you can link these to a subdomain on your website such that they have a similar address and feel part of your site. The data they capture should go directly into your CRM or mailing list.

If you have review management software set up then this is an excellent place to use those review widgets as well – providing social proof that you're as good as you claim to be.

Chatbots

Increasingly the interactions between cold leads at the top of your marketing funnel and you happen via the medium of chat, and direct messaging services such as Facebook Messenger and WhatsApp have become essential tools for every small business to communicate with leads and clients alike.

The "always-on" nature of social media, and the ability for leads to contact you at any time of day or night regardless of whether or not they understand whether you can help them with their problem can be overwhelming for many small business owners, and particularly difficult for therapists.

One of the areas where automation can help is by using a simple chatbot attached to your Facebook page or your WhatsApp account to deal with the most basic queries. For example, if someone simply wants to know how to book with you, a chatbot can understand that's what they want, and it can guide them to the right page on your website or your online diary and ensure that they simply and efficiently arrive where they need to go. Alternatively, if someone approaches you because they've seen some of your social media content and they want to know a bit more about the therapies that you offer, it can direct them to blogs or articles you've written, which might be relevant, or to your YouTube channel to watch some videos.

Maybe there are common questions that many of your prospective clients ask, in which case the chatbot could provide them with simple answers. This may allow them to determine whether or not your therapy is a good fit for their problem or it may help them understand your pricing structure. It might help also you to qualify or disqualify leads as being someone that you can help, or not.

You can think of a chatbot as a great big decision tree where every question has a number of available answers and, depending upon the answer, selected the conversation will be steered down a specific route. It will take some time to set up but a well-engineered chatbot can answer a high proportion of the simple queries that come in from the coldest leads.

Of course, you'll never want to use a chatbot, as a substitute for you speaking directly to one of your clients, but perhaps you could use a chatbot to help someone who wants to know more about what you do or to find the article that they need that will help them to understand whether you can help them or not.

It's through this educational role that chatbot can really shine. I've talked previously about how the top of your funnel leads are Problem Unaware and then they become

Problem Aware, but it takes some time before they become Solution Aware and realise that they have a problem and you are the solution. On that journey, a chatbot can help to move them through some of those stages and can help them to understand what symptoms or issues they may have, may indicate they have the problem that you're an expert in solving, or that they don't have that problem, in which case they need to find the right expert for them.

It will not resolve 100% of your inbound queries, any more than having a website or writing an article resolves 100% of them, but you can think about it as an interactive set of articles. If you like it's a little bit like the "Choose Your Own Adventure" books that you may have read as a teenager, but where the "adventure" is your body of knowledge and published articles. By automatically directing cold leads to your marketing materials, which are most appropriate for their needs, they will be able to most quickly become Problem Aware and then Solution Aware and either become your client or disqualify themselves, saving you time from having long conversations with people who ultimately you can't help.

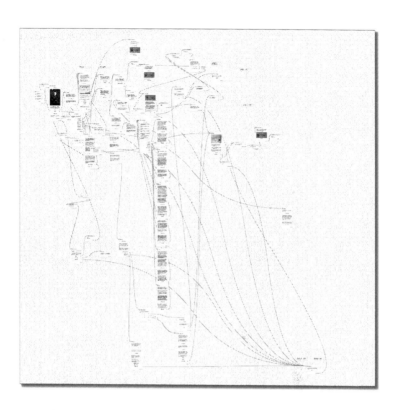

It may look daunting at first but building a chatbot is surprisingly easy

Properly implemented a chatbot means that by the time a prospective client reaches the Discovery Call stage of your process and you speak to them, there's a good chance they'll already know what questions you need to ask and what questions they need to ask, and you'll be able to have a much more focused and productive conversation, establish whether or not you feel you can work together and agree a plan going forward, rather than spending a proportion of that time explaining the basics, over and over again.

If you have a large body of video material, where you talk about many of the issues and questions that a lead will need to know the answers to, then a chatbot is even better because it can guide them through that video experience, and hear you talk in your own words about what they need to know. It will give them the majority of what they would get from a face to face conversation with you, but it will do that without consuming large quantities of your time on an ongoing basis to deliver. Even better, it will do that, whether it's 3 pm on a Wednesday, or 3 am on a Sunday, whether you're busy, whether you're working, whether you're sleeping. It will allow a lead to go through the journey to becoming your client at their own pace, in their own timescales, in a manner that suits them. You only need to record all of this information once to make that happen.

So chatbots can be enormously powerful tools. They do need to be set up properly, however, because they can also be horribly impersonal, and there are many poor implementations of chatbots out there already. Done right, however, they will save time in your business, and they will give your client, a better experience.

A tool I use within my business is Manychat. Manychat is a platform that is primarily geared around Facebook Messenger, which works well for me because Facebook Messenger is where the majority of my inbound conversational messages are delivered to me. Of course, if you use other platforms such as WhatsApp primarily, you will need to consider other software. However, if you're primarily using Facebook Messenger then Manychat is a good option and is relatively inexpensive. It has a very good visual conversation builder and works in a robust and resilient way.

It can direct users to content hosted elsewhere on the web, including videos, and web pages as well as being able to provide answers and content directly within the conversations. The conversations themselves get tracked through the Facebook business pages application, and available for you to review later on and Manychat can also be integrated with your CRM platform to ensure that you capture the lead, and their details, and can follow up at an appropriate time, either automatically or manually depending on the nature of the conversation. The Chatbot can also place leads into your standard email funnel, if that's appropriate, or it can just deliver content directly to them in real-time during the conversation oriented (or it can do both).

For existing clients, you could use a chatbot to help them to understand information, like, what type of follow up appointment they need to book or help them to more quickly navigate your website to find information such as prices, booking details, etc.

One point to note, if you're using Facebook Messenger is that Facebook does not allow the integration of chatbots or any other third party tools to your personal account you will need to have a business page. And we need to use the Messenger account associated with our business page. However, once you have that in place, a well designed, chatbot will save you time and money in your business.

16 Return On

Investment

So you've seen the areas where you could reduce or eliminate wasted time in your business and you're probably keen to get started. Maybe you're worried about the costs of all of this though.

Ensuring that you get a return on investment (ROI) is essential when introducing automation and process re-engineering.

Unless you can be sure you more than covered your costs with the savings or extra income (i.e. you got a positive ROI) then you haven't achieved your objective.

The safest way to ensure a positive ROI is to introduce these changes incrementally. Pick an area where you have the highest waste and solve that first. Check that you've achieved a positive ROI for that piece before proceeding.

If you have not then it's vital you understand why – because you just made your business less competitive, not more!

Of course, there are two ways to get a positive ROI – get a really big return, or make a really small investment.

This is the other benefit of breaking things down – the investment is smaller, which means the hurdle to make it beneficial to your business is lower.

You can take this further – if you consider the free options on many pieces of software mentioned here, you'll realise that you can get a good chunk of the functionality on the free plans. Implementing this is a good stepping stone. Your main cost here is probably your own time (and don't forget that when you do the calculation – as the main way your business makes money, it's far from free!) and if you can show a positive ROI at low cost, then you can consider the incremental ROI of moving to a paid plan, with the benefit of much better understanding on the benefits that might bring.

You will need to be able to quantify the benefits and to do that, you'll need to understand metrics like how much is one appointment is worth to you (it's going to be different for different businesses but at the time of writing, the average therapist across all therapies across all of the UK is about £62 for an hourly appointment).

That's our best guess of what saving an hour a week might be worth to you, and knowing that is pivotal in working out whether an investment is going to be worthwhile. Once you've made a change, understanding the return that you got from each change you made is the Analyse phase that I talked about earlier in the book and it is important that you do it, to check that your assumptions were valid when starting and be sure that you succeeded in improving the efficiency of your business.

Most software will give you a 14 to 30-day free trial, but the important thing is what the ongoing costs will look like after that ends. The trial is the time to satisfy yourself it can work, and configure it but always calculate the ROI based on the normal operating cost. Some tools have free-forever plans, others do not. Be realistic about which features you need to make it work though.

For example, for the online calendar system, you can take a tool like Calendly which has a free plan. If you don't mind their branding being on it, and you only one appointment type, and don't want to take online payment, it is (currently) completely free. However, you need to consider whether within those constraints it works meaningfully in your business, even as an experiment. You could end up doing just as much, or more, work because of the limitations, which would disappear if you spent £10 per month and might free up an additional hour or more.

Similarly, with CRM systems, HubSpot, if you take some feature restrictions, you can use absolutely free. However, if you do need to move to the paid plan, you can find yourself committed to well above the entry-level headline price if you have accrued a large list of contacts, even for just adding a single feature.

The one place where there is a pretty unavoidable cost is the online payment system. I would certainly recommend Stripe over PayPal because PayPal is nearly twice as expensive. Stripe is 1.4% plus $0.30 per transaction, whilst PayPal is 2.9% plus $0.20. So, that's potentially going to cost you maybe £1-2 on an appointment depending on what your appointment fee is.

But think about that, in the context of how much time potentially you're saving here. I would argue that there are very few businesses for which 1.4% is cost-effective to do manually unless you are the fastest, least error-prone typist that has ever lived.

Some Example Scenarios

By now you'll see that there is a huge range of options to pick from but to give some order of magnitude on the costs, let's think about a couple of scenarios.

Clinic with 3 therapists

If you had a clinic with three therapists, with 1000 clients, and wanted to completely automate all of this it is reasonable to estimate this costing around £250 per month.

So that's probably a little over one hour per therapist per month in terms of time.

Solo Therapist

If you are a solo therapist and wanted to fully automate your business, with about 100 clients, it is reasonable to estimate this costing around £120 per month - probably about 2 hours per month in terms of time.

17 Summary

Hopefully, by now you can see where I was going with the title and my comments at the beginning of this book around wasting time.

I'm absolutely not suggesting the being in a therapy business is wasting your time - I am however suggesting that many therapists waste time in their business. As you've worked through this book and looked at your own business processes you will have started to see where that might be the case for you.

No one goes into business because they love doing administration - even virtual assistants who do administration generally have not gone into business because they want to do their own administration! Certainly, if you've spent time, effort and money qualifying as a highly-skilled therapist, you surely do not want to spend time doing administration.

Using the skills that I hope you've learned, as you've read through this book, combined with the practical advice around software platforms that can help you, I hope you have found opportunities within your own business to streamline your processes, reorder and simplify them, remove unnecessary steps and generally, improve your clients' experience, and to combine that with some properly thought through software choices, which will allow you to remove some of that burden of administration.

I hope that having got this far, you can start to see that my promise of three weeks on the beach in the introduction, might just be achievable for you.

However, Rome wasn't built in a day, and your business will not be transformed in a day, or with a single reading of a book. Transforming your business will take time, and I would always advise people to pick one area at a time and get that working well, before moving on to the next one, otherwise you risk overwhelming yourself. If things don't quite go to plan and you've changed too much in one go, it can be really difficult to work out which part needs some tweaking.

If having read all of this, you're now keen to get started, I, therefore, urge you to revisit my thoughts in the chapter on planning... break it down into bite-sized pieces and decide which piece you're going to change first. Once you've decided on that, and you've made that change, give it a chance to bed down before moving on to the next part.

New tools, new systems and new processes will take you time to become comfortable and competent with, but once you do become comfortable and competent with them they will save you an enormous amount of time and stress. So use the tools and techniques you've learned in this book, as the beginning of your continuous improvement journey in your business. Even once you think you have fixed everything you can fix, and your business is running perfectly, keep asking...

"Why am I doing this?"

"What's the benefit of doing this?"

"How could I do this quicker, easier, better?"

"How could I provide the same service to my client, with less effort for me less cost for me and a better outcome for them?"

Not least because the software landscape is constantly changing, and the advice I give in this book is valid at the time of writing (April 2021) but if there's one thing I can guarantee it's that in 12 months, two years, five years, 10 years there will be all sorts of other capabilities available that will allow you to do things that right now seem unimaginable for a small business. Those who embrace those new capabilities will be the ones whose businesses grow and thrive, and who can balance their business and their lifestyle, in the way that they want to. Whereas those who do not will become under increasing pressure of time and income, and will be working harder and harder to stand still.

So what you've learned in this book is not a destination. It is simply the beginning of a journey. It's a journey that many other therapists have taken or will be taking (and some may not realise they need to). As with many journeys, they're much easier and more interesting if you bring friends so gather a community around you. Have other similar minded, professionals, work together, bounce ideas off each other, talk about what worked and what didn't work and why it worked or didn't work. Something you try that completely fails to save you time and effort in your business might work incredibly well for a colleague and a different discipline, and vice versa. But the only way to know that is to talk about it, and have the conversation, and then try it and be bold and see whether you can make it work.

The robots are indeed coming... they're coming to save us. They're coming to save us from tedium and boredom and to free us to spend our time on things we love doing. But using them wisely will require new skills and an open mind.

Therapists are hugely well placed to benefit from this technology over the next decade. We're many, many years away from a point where AI and robotics can come close to matching human therapists, skill, compassion and empathy. However, we are reaching the point where AI can free therapists up to spend all their time, using those things, and none of their time crunching numbers, copying, pasting, playing telephone tennis and trying to keep track of client notes or bits of paper.

The technology is here with us now and it's affordable for every small business. I urge you to embrace it and to find a way that it will allow you to do what you love and ...

automate what you hate!

18 About The Author

I have over 26 years of experience in business automation and change, and data management and systems and have work with businesses of all sizes.

I help businesses to consider processes and culture as well as implementing the technology to help them avoid the pitfalls that 70% of organisations fall into and fail at change.

- Identify the critical bottlenecks in a business

- Develop a commercially sensible IT strategy for businesses and help them to implement it

- Integrate all of the systems they have and introduce automation

- Develop reporting and dashboards to allow owners to understand and monitor the health of their business

Join my Facebook group:

https://www.facebook.com/groups/GrowYourBusinessWithoutWorkingHarder

My *Business Automation Academy* is a membership programme for small business owners who want to learn the skills they need to transform their businesses with technology and automation.

You can find out more at **https://learn.cobaltbeach.com**

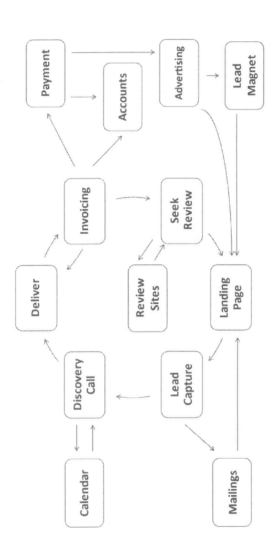

Printed in Great Britain
by Amazon